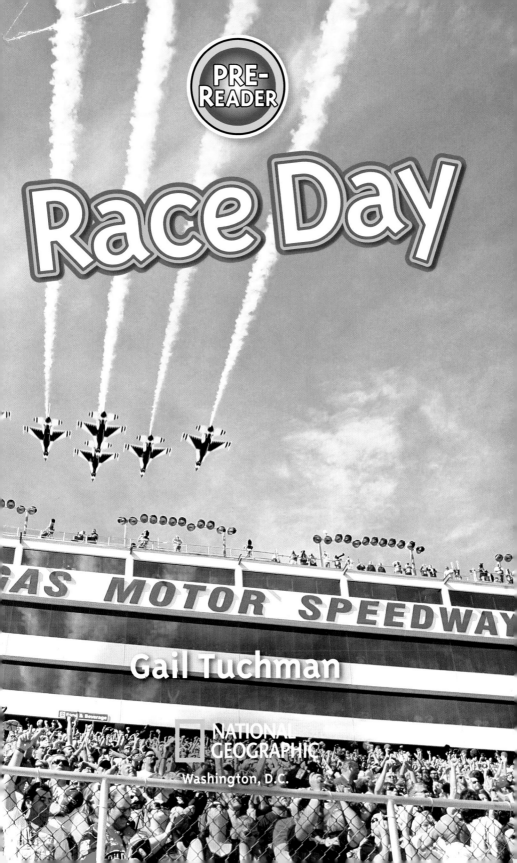

PRE-READER

Race Day

Gail Tuchman

NATIONAL GEOGRAPHIC
Washington, D.C.

For Lauren Hope—G.T.

Copyright © 2010 National Geographic Society

Published by the National Geographic Society, Washington, D.C. 20036. All rights reserved.
Reproduction in whole or in part without written permission of the publisher is prohibited.

Library of Congress Cataloging-in-Publication Data
Tuchman, Gail.
Race day / by Gail Tuchman.
p. cm.
ISBN 978-1-4263-0612-9 (trade pbk. : alk. paper) -- ISBN 978-1-4263-0613-6 (library binding : alk. paper)
1. Automobile racing--Juvenile literature. I. Title.
GV1029.13.T83 2010
796.72--dc22
2009006126

Cover: © Chris Graythen/Getty Images; 1: © Aaron Josefczyk/Icon SMI/Corbis; 2, 5 (bottom): © Don Kelly Photo/Corbis; 3: © PatrickSchneiderPhoto.com; 4: © Robert Lesieur/Reuters/Corbis; 5 (top), 13: © Jonathan Ferrey/Getty Images; 6: © Jerry Markland/Getty Images for NASCAR; 7 (top): © M. Timothy O'Keefe/Alamy; 7 (bottom): © Jon Feingersh/Stone/Getty Images; 8: © AP Photo/Jamie Squire, Pool; 9: © Fred Vuich/Sports Illustrated/Getty Images; 10-11, 14, 24: © George Tiedemann/GT Images/Corbis; 12: © AP Photo/Dave Martin; 15: © David Wei/Alamy; 16-17: © Ronald Martinez/Getty Images for NASCAR; 18: © Matthew T. Thacker/ASP./Icon SMI/Corbis; 20-21: © Frank Whitney/Stone/Getty Images; 22: © Brand X Pictures/Getty Images; 23: © AP Photo/Steve Helber.

National Geographic supports K—12 educators with ELA Common Core Resources.
Visit natgeoed.org/commoncore for more information.

Collection ISBN (Paperback): 978-1-4263-1972-3
Collection ISBN (Library Edition): 978-1-4263-1973-0

Printed in China
14/RRDS/1

Vroom! Vroom!

Cars ZOOM
on race day.

Gear up. Climb inside.
Ready to ride?

Pull into your row.
The green flag is waving GO!

Ride round the turn.

Tires burn as cars ZOOM
on race day.

Lap after lap,
fans cheer and clap
as cars ZOOM
on race day.

Pit stops.
Tire swaps.
The crew hops.

Tires burn as cars ZOOM.

Vroom! Vroom! On race day.

Hot on your tail,
a car hangs tight.

You can't go left.
You can't go right.

Foot down! Pick up speed.

Blast past. You're in the lead.

ZOOM past the flag
to take first place.

VROOM! VROOM!

You win the race…
on race day.

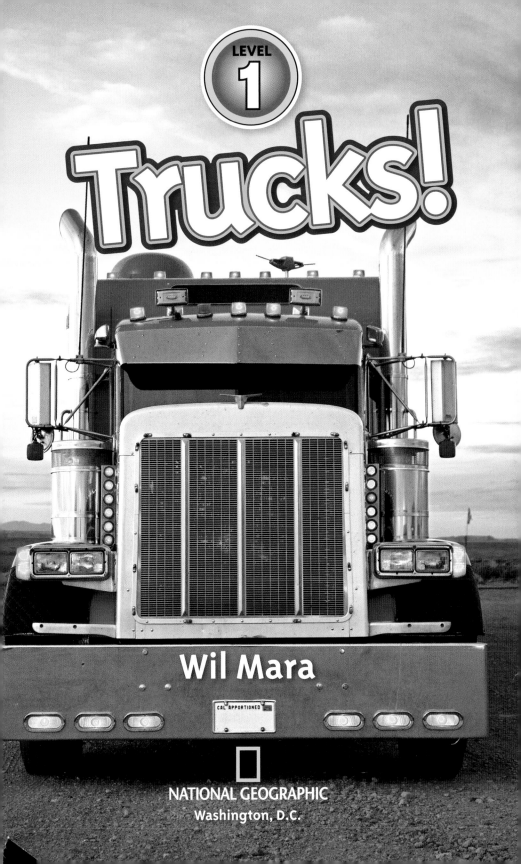

LEVEL
1

Trucks!

Wil Mara

NATIONAL GEOGRAPHIC
Washington, D.C.

For Andy and Scott, who know more
about trucks than I ever will. — W.M.

Published by the National Geographic Society, Washington, D.C. 20036. All rights reserved.
Reproduction in whole or in part without written permission of the publisher is prohibited.

Library of Congress Cataloging-in-Publication Data
Mara, Wil.
Trucks / Wil Mara.
p. cm.
ISBN 978-1-4263-0526-9 (paperback : alk. paper) -- ISBN 978-1-4263-0527-6 (library binding : alk. paper)
1. Trucks--Juvenile literature. I. Title.
TL230.15.M366 2009
629.225--dc22
2009021037

All photos of "Slick" © Mark Thiessen/NationalGeographicStock.com; Cover: © Walter Hodges/ Photographer's Choice/
Getty Images; 1: © Christopher Thomas/ Photographer's Choice/ Getty Images; 2: © Code Red/ Getty Images; 5: © Brian
Sullivan; 6-7, 32 (top, left): © Lester Lefkowitz/ Stone/ Getty Images; 8-9: © Alain Le Bot/ Photolibrary; 10: © AP Photo/ Pat
Sullivan; 12-13: © Guy Crittenden/ Photographer's Choice RF/ Getty Images; 14-15: © Donald R. Swartz/ Shutterstock; 16-17:
© Daniel Valla FRPS/ Alamy; 17 (right inset), 32 (bottom, left): © age footstock/ SuperStock; 18-19: © Scott Olson/ Getty
Images; 20-21: © Ian Dagnall/ Alamy; 22-23: © Stuart Walker/ Alamy; 24-25: © Joe Baraban/ Transtock/ JupiterImages;
26-27: © Fernando Rodrigues/ Shutterstock; 28-29, 32 (bottom, right): © Robert Kerian/ Transtock/ Alamy; 30: © Richard
Leeney/ Dorling Kindersley/ DK Images; 32 (top, right): © Dorling Kindersley/ Getty Images.

Table of Contents

Meet Slick

Hi, I'm Slick.
Do you like trucks?
I sure do. Big or small,
I like them ALL!

Dump Truck

A dump truck carries sand, rocks, and dirt. The back of the truck is like a big box.

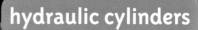

hydraulic cylinders

Two hydraulic cylinders push the box up and **Whoosh!** the load spills out.

Say *Hi-draw-lik sil-en-ders.*

TRUCK TALK

Hydraulic Cylinders: Tubes filled with oil

Tow Truck

Oh, no. This car needs a ride. A tow truck pushes its flat bed to the street. Chains hook to the axle of the car and pull it onto the bed. They hold it tight for a ride to the shop.

Garbage Truck

hydraulic cylinder

Garbage trucks have major mojo! This front loader lifts a big trash bin. Up and over goes the garbage. It is tipped in, crunched back, smushed and pushed.

Check out these hydraulics!

209073

MACK

Cement Mixer

The best part of a cement mixer is the drum. If it's rolling, the truck has new cement inside. The drum cannot stop rolling. If it does, the cement will harden in the drum.

Fire Truck

There are all kinds of fire trucks. This one is a pump truck. It pumps water. It has hoses and a water cannon.

A pump truck hooks up to a hydrant to get water.

water cannon

www.kearnyusa.com

Tanker Truck

A tanker truck carries fluid, like milk. There is a hatch on top of the tank, where the tank is filled.

TRUCK TALK

Hatch: The door that covers a small opening.

hatch

hatch

first milk

17

Car Transport

How cool is this?

It's a car transport.

upper deck

It carries new cars on its trailer. The trailer has upper decks and a lower deck. The upper decks are lifted by hydraulics.

Check it out! Hydraulics!

lower deck

An armored truck has a bulletproof shell. Even the windows and tires are bulletproof.

Heavy Hauler

Some trucks have big jobs.

Sometimes they even carry other trucks!

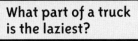
A heavy hauler carries big things, like houses and airplanes. It needs a lot of wheels. These trucks are also called 18-wheelers.

BANKS

BANKS

TV139

BANKS BROS.

Phone
01740
658500

STGO
CAT 3

NX55 ATN

Liebherr T282

This is one of the biggest trucks in the world. It's a dump truck. The driver has to climb a ladder just to get into the seat! It also has video cameras so the driver can see on all sides. It can carry more than 50 schoolbuses. This truck costs 3 million dollars!

Slick's Big Rig

Here is my rig.
It is a tractor trailer.
The tractor part is
the front. It pulls
the trailer.

Slick's Office

speedometer

TRUCK TALK

Dashboard:
Where all
the controls
for the truck
are found

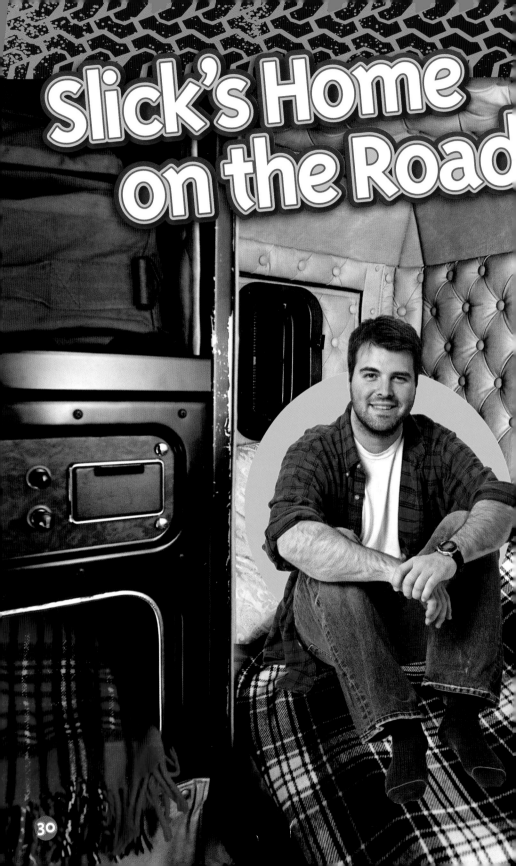

Slick's Home on the Road

I can pull off the road and sleep in my cab. This is my home away from home. I love my truck!

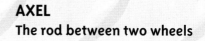

HYDRAULIC CYLINDERS
Tubes filled with oil

AXEL
The rod between two wheels

HATCH
The door that covers
a small opening

DASHBOARD
Where all the controls for the
truck are found

LEVEL 1

Planes

Amy Shields

NATIONAL GEOGRAPHIC

Washington, D.C.

For Jenny, who hates to fly. — A.S.

Published by the National Geographic Society, Washington, D.C. 20036. All rights reserved.
Reproduction in whole or in part without written permission of the publisher is prohibited.

Library of Congress Cataloging-in-Publication Data

Shields, Amy.
Planes / by Amy Shields.
p. cm.
ISBN 978-1-4263-0712-6 (pbk. : alk. paper) -- ISBN 978-1-4263-0713-3 (library binding : alk. paper)
1. Airplanes--Juvenile literature. I. Title.
TL547.S5135 2010
629.133'34--dc22
2010011648

All photos of "Pilot Nic" by Becky Hale/National Geographic Staff; Cover, Robert Marien/ Corbis; 1, Kurt Rogers/ San
Francisco Chronicle/ Corbis; 2, Terrance Klassen/ Photolibrary; 4, Marcel Jolibois/ Photononstop/ Photolibrary; 6, Scott
Stulberg/ Corbis; 8, Georgios Alexandris/ Shutterstock; 10, Terry Mitchell/ US Air Force/ Department of Defense; 12, MSGT
Pat Nugent/ Department of Defense; 14, Robin Starr; 15, Staff Sgt. James Selesnick/ US Army; 17, Judson Brohmer/ USAF/
NASA; 18, AFP/ AFP/ Getty Images; 19 (top), Jenzinho/ Shutterstock; 19, Ian Waldie/ Bloomberg/ Getty Images; 21, Dwight
Smith/ Shutterstock; 22, 24 Mass Communication Specialist Seaman Brandon Morris/ US Navy; 25, Mass Communication
Specialist 2nd Class Milosz Reterski/ US Navy; 26, Gary Ell/ US Navy; 28, Fotosearch/ Getty Images; 31, Buyenlarge/ Getty
Images; 32 (top, left), Fotosearch/ Getty Images; 32 (top, right), Staff Sgt. James Selesnick/ US Army; 32 (middle, left), Mass
Communication Specialist Seaman Brandon Morris/ US Navy; 32 (middle, right), Dwight Smith/ Shutterstock; 32 (bottom,
left), Mass Communication Specialist 1st Class Heather Ewton/ US Navy; 32 (bottom, right), Judson Brohmer/ USAF/ NASA.

Table of Contents

Flying High

There are seatbelts but no steering wheel. There is no gas pedal. Where are we? We are in the cockpit of an airplane.

Hi! I am pilot Nic. Welcome aboard!

The pilot sits in the cockpit. We sit in the cabin. The cabin has TVs in the seats. It has bathrooms. It has a kitchen so we can have a snack. It is just like home, but 30,000 feet in the air.

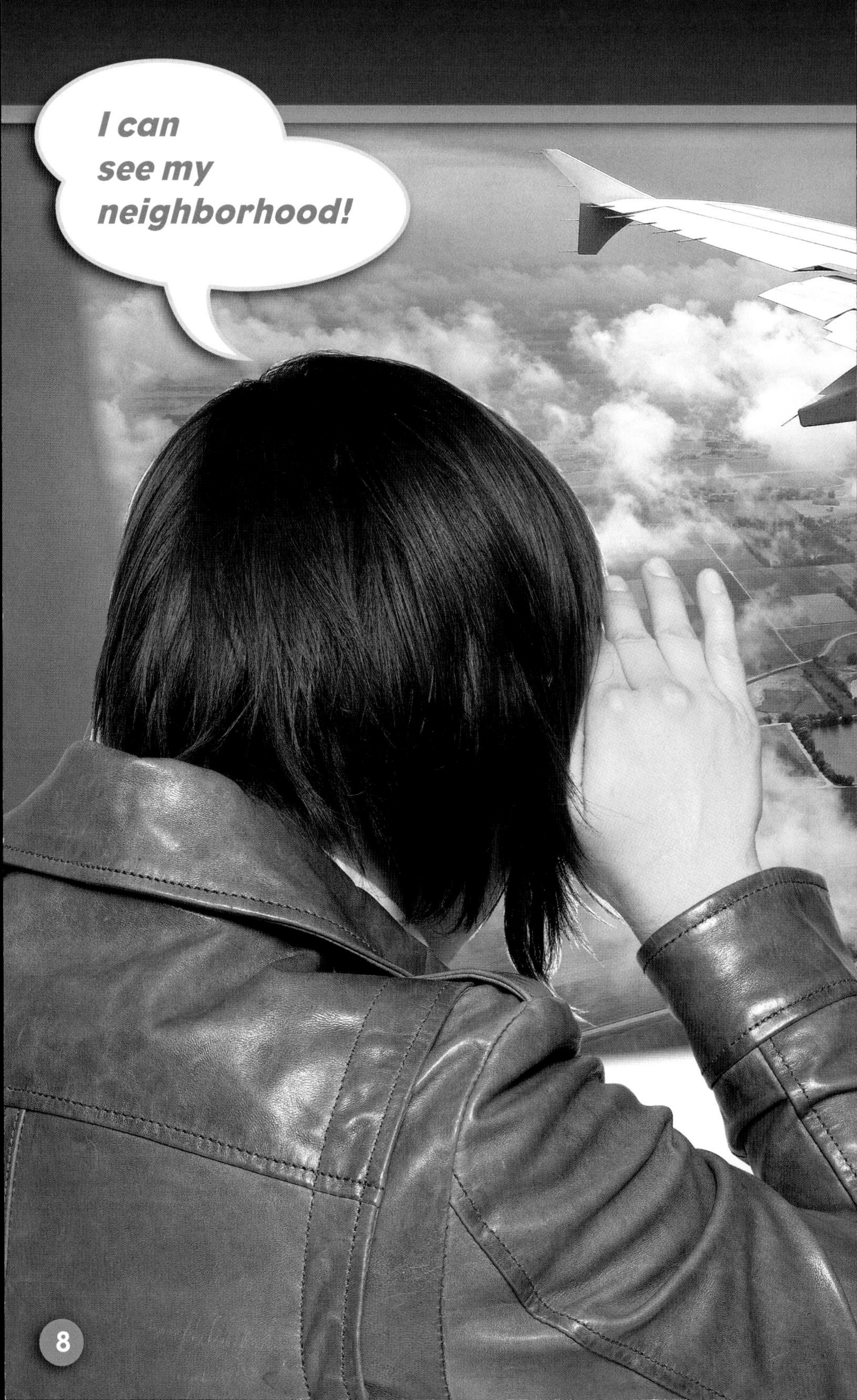
I can see my neighborhood!

Q | Why did the elephant take so long to get to the airport?

A | Because he had to pack his trunk.

Look out the window. From above, the Earth looks like a quilt of fields, forests, cities, and towns.

Some planes do not have TVs or snacks. They are working planes. This is the inside of a C-17 Globemaster. It carries a mobile home bolted to the floor. VIPs go in here to talk in private.

Some planes are built to carry stuff. Big stuff. This is the Antonov 225. It is the biggest plane ever made. It is so big and heavy it needs 32 wheels to land.

You can drive 80 cars into the belly of this plane.

Flying Bees

Bumble Bee I

The smallest plane used to be the Bumble Bee. It is 9½ feet long. Then came the Bumble Bee II. It was about a foot shorter.

There are even smaller planes, but they are not for people. This is a drone. It is flown by remote control.

Wing Words

DRONE: A plane driven by remote control

Fast and Fancy

The fastest plane is the SR-71 Blackbird. Only two people fit in this plane. It flies 3,418 miles an hour.

The SR-71 is a spy plane. Shhhhh!

Q *Do you know which plane brought this boomerang?*

Some planes are plain.
Some are painted.

Long ago some pilots painted their planes with scary faces. These planes are called Flying Tigers. They were flown in World War II.

City on the Sea

I'm here, you just can't see me!

Most planes leave the ground from a runway. But sometimes the runway is in the middle of the ocean. The U.S.S. *Enterprise* is an aircraft carrier. It carries 70 airplanes, 5,000 people, and enough cooks to make 15,000 meals a day!

Wing Words

JET: An engine that uses a stream of gases to make the plane fly

The runway on the *Enterprise* is 20 stories above the ocean. Planes take off into the air from the deck. They go from 0 to 165 miles an hour in 2 seconds!

Landing is just as hard. Each plane has a tailhook. The hook catches on a wire to stop the plane. These pilots have nerves of steel.

These are jet airplanes.

Flying Gas Station

Wing Words

STEALTH: Secret, undercover

B-2 Stealth Bomber

Here is another pilot with nerves of steel. The little plane is a B-2 stealth bomber. The pilot is filling his gas tank while he is flying in the air!

Refueling tanker
say: ree-few-ling

Fill'er up!

The First

Orville Wright

Wilbur Wright

Anemometer
say: Ann-ee-MOM-ee-t...

Wing Words

ANEMOMETER: A tool for measuring wind speed

The Wright brothers were brave, too. They were the first to fly a plane. That was more than 100 years ago, but we still remember them. They were smart and unafraid, and they did it first. Hooray!

Take to the Sky

One hundred years before the Wright Brothers, someone else was dreaming of flying. But this balloon was never built, so no one ever flew it.

What are you dreaming about?

"La Minerve"
Vaisseau Aérien destiné aux Decouvertes
1803

ANEMOMETER: A tool for measuring wind speed

DRONE: A plane driven by remote control

JET: An engine that uses a stream of gases to make the plane fly

PROPELLER: An engine that tur blades to make the plane fly

STEALTH: Secret, undercover

VIP: Very Important Person

Trains

708 708

SANTA FE

Amy Shields

NATIONAL
GEOGRAPHIC
Washington, D.C.

To the Silver Star, Empire, Vermonter, and Adirondack trains, long may they run. — A.S.

Text copyright © 2011 National Geographic Society
Published by the National Geographic Society, Washington, D.C. 20036. All rights reserved.
Reproduction in whole or in part without written permission of the publisher is prohibited.

All photos of Gary the Engineer by Becky Hale/ NationalGeographicStock.com

Library of Congress Cataloging-in-Publication Data

Shields, Amy.
Trains / by Amy Shields.
p. cm.—(National geographic readers)
ISBN 978-1-4263-0777-5 (pbk. : alk. paper)—ISBN 978-1-4263-0778-2
(library binding : alk. paper)
1. Railroads—United States—History—Juvenile literature. 2. Railroad
travel—United States—History—Juvenile literature. I. Title.
TF23.S54 2011
625.1—dc22
2010050659

Table of Contents

Lots of Trains

Steam train, freight train,
circus train, cold train.

Grain train, coal train,
people-on-the-go train.

All Aboard!

Have you been on a steam train ride? Did you hear the wheels clackety-clack on the track? Did you hear the WOOOO-woo whistle? Did the ding-ding-ding bell ring at the train crossing?

I'm Gary and this is my train. I am the engineer.

Train Talk

ENGINEER: A person who drives the train

Full Steam Ahead

Steam trains have noisy, moving parts.

Heat from burning coal or oil turns water into steam. The steam moves the pistons.

The pistons move the rods. The rods turn the wheels and move the train on the tracks.

rod

Trains have special wheels that roll on tracks. Most train tracks are made of steel rails and wood ties. The rails are nailed to the ties.

Trains follow tracks over valleys.

They roll on tracks through mountains.

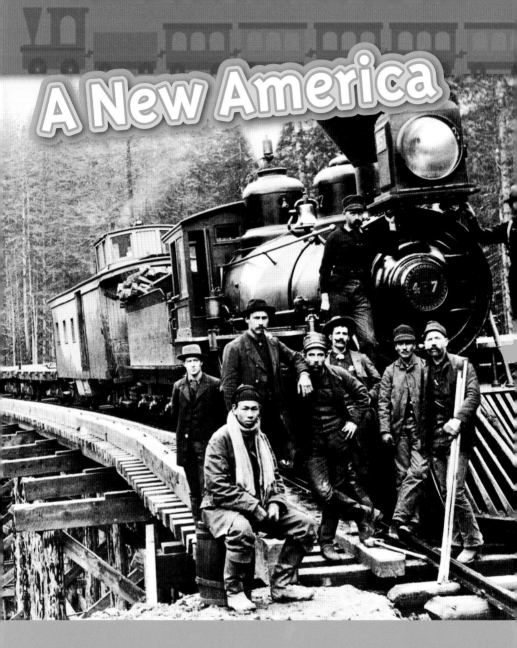

A New America

About 150 years ago, Chinese and Irish people helped build the train tracks. They became new Americans.

When the tracks were done, they stretched across America. More people moved west. Towns were built along the rail tracks. Banks and stores were built. Trains brought them money and gold.

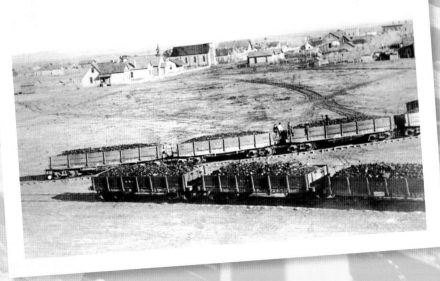

Many trains got held up by robbers.

Robbers wanted to steal the money and gold. Butch Cassidy and the Sundance Kid were robbers. They robbed trains with their gang. Then they rode off on their horses. They split the loot at their hideout, the Hole-in-the-Wall.

Train Talk

LOOT: Stolen money and gold

Cool Things About Trains

1
Some bullet trains float magnetically above the rails.

2
The Fairy Queen in India is one of the oldest running steam trains.

EIR 22

3
People who love trains are called railfans. They take vacations to go trainspotting.

The longest train tunnel in the world is 35 miles long. It goes through the Alps mountains. It will open in 2017.

4

5

Many train stations are called Union Station. These are stations used by different train lines.

6

A puppy was found on a mail car in 1888. The mailmen named him Owney. He rode the mail trains and became their lucky charm.

Train Tricks

What happens when trains reach the end of the track? Tracks in a rail yard lead to a turntable. The locomotive rolls onto the turntable.

Whirrrrr. The turntable turns. The locomotive rolls off in a new direction.

Train Talk

TURNTABLE:
A piece of train track that can be turned

A turntable is a cool train invention. Here are more cool inventions. People thought of ways to ride train tracks even without trains.

Look at some of these inventions.

mule-drawn train car

handcar

21

Passenger Trains

Now there are train tracks all over the world.

People take trains to get to work. They take train ride vacations, too.

The Maharajas' Express is a train in India. It is called a palace on wheels.

It was built for royalty. People take vacations on this train. It is a nice, slow ride through the country.

Want a faster ride? Bullet trains
are fast like bullets. These trains
go more than 275 miles an hour.
Bullet trains run on train tracks.

Some bullet trains are pulled by
locomotives. Some have motors for
each car. Bullet trains are passenger
trains, for people.

Bullet trains are electric. They have pantographs on top of some of the cars. Wires overhead pass electricity to the pantographs.

pantograph

Train Talk

PANTOGRAPH: Metal arms on a train's roof that catch electricity from wires above

Say *PAN-toe-graf*

Electricity comes from coal, the same coal that powers steam engines.

Freight Trains

Freight trains carry stuff, like sneakers and cell phones. The longest freight trains are two miles long. These trains have diesel locomotives. The locomotives in front pull. The locomotives in back push.

Most of the stuff in your house rode on a train at one time.

Say *DEE-zul*

diesel locomotive

9004

9004

9004

PTW
8

When trains roll past, railmen
stand aside and watch. Next time
a train passes you, wave hi to the
mighty train rolling clackety-clack
down the track.

ENGINEER: A person who drives the train

LOOT: Stolen money and gold

PANTOGRAPH: Metal arms on a train's roof that catch electricity from wires above

TURNTABLE: A piece of train track that can be turned

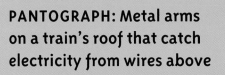